Table of Contents

Introduction

Many people want to eat healthy but they do not have the time to cook their own food. Thus, they resort to take outs and fast-food items. The problem with this particular diet and way of eating is that people eat unhealthy and processed foods, which may lead to metabolic diseases like high blood pressure, stroke, and diabetes.

Now would it be nice to be able to cook your meals despite your busy schedule? The answer lies with the Instant Pot. A revolutionary digital pressure cooker, the Instant Pot works similarly with an ordinary pressure cooker but unlike an ordinary pressure cooker, it has pre-set buttons that remove the guesswork in your cooking. This allows you to cook different types of foods from meat, fish, poultry, and even grains. Thus, saving you money as you don't have to buy other cookware to make other dishes.

Whole Foods

What are Whole Foods? Whole Foods are essentially fresh and unprocessed foods, hence the term "Whole." Whole Foods is also known as foods as close to their natural form as possible. They do not contain preservatives like chemicals, salt, or even sugars to lengthen their shelf life. So, to make it easy, whole foods are fresh. The only exception to this rule would be dairy products because these go through the pasteurization process—but it doesn't even adulterate the food. It just removes bacteria in the milk to ensure it does not go rancid right away.

So, what's the deal with whole foods? With so many health issues pestering us nowadays, more and more people have embraced healthy living, healthy cooking, and healthy eating. A lot of people, as well as scientists, believe that most of the health issues that we experience are brought about by our unhealthy food choices and that we are advised to steer clear of these "fast and highly-processed foods." And that's how the Whole Foods movement was born.

So, how do you easily embark on a Whole Foods Diet? Simple! Read on...

- When drinking, choose healthy options like soy or skim milk, fresh fruit juice, green tea, or good old plain water. No sugary drinks!
- Avoid highly processed foods like frozen dinners or fast food for convenience' sake.
- Add more beans in your diet. They are a good source of nutrients, fiber, phytochemicals, and protein.

- Eat a LOT of fresh fruits and vegetables.
- When buying grains, always opt for 100% whole grains.

You can cook healthy and delicious meals from whole food ingredients with Instant Pot. Cooking foods using whole food ingredients is very easy with Instant Pot plus you get a lot of benefits from eating nutrient-dense foods packed with antioxidants and enzymes. In fact, eating whole foods can help reduce the likelihood of developing diabetes, high blood pressure, and obesity.

And so, with Instant Pot, you will be able to benefit from eating healthy and you will have no excuse not to eat healthy and delicious meals every single day.

Chapter 1: Instant Pot

It might be overwhelming to use the Instant Pot but it is a very straightforward digital pressure cooker that allows you to cook different types of foods using its reset buttons. The secret of cooking successfully with the Instant Pot is knowing how its button work. Thus, this chapter will discuss about the many buttons of the Instant Pot and their functions.

Main Buttons

The main buttons of the Instant Pot are found on the control panel. These buttons allow you to make adjustments on your Instant Pot as well as use this particular kitchen appliance for other purposes. Below are the main buttons of the Instant Pot.

- **Slow cook:** The best thing about the Instant Pot is that it does not only work as a pressure cooker but also a slow cooker. When you press this button, it has a preset cooking time of 4 hours but you can adjust the cooking time by pressing the + or − button. Moreover, you can change the cooking temperature so that your food cooks more slowly.

- **Adjust:** This particular button allows you to change the temperature setting so that you can customize the amount of temperature that your food is being cooked in.
- **Sauté:** Unlike other pressure cooker, the Instant Pot comes with a sauté button that allows you to sauté spices as well as simmer food to thicken sauces. The sauté button has a default temperature range of 320°F to 349°F. To use this button, simply press it but don't ever close the lid so that it does not build any pressure.
- **Yogurt:** You can turn the Instant Pot as a yogurt machine so that you can turn dairy into added-value yogurt. Aside from yogurt, you can also use this setting to make different types of fermented foods.
- **Manual:** Perhaps one of the most important button of all, the Manual button allows you to cook food at a temperature setting that you want.
- **Timer:** This particular button allows you to set how long you want your food to be cooked. It also functions as a delayed timer so you can cook your food at a specified time at a later moment.
- **Pressure:** Choose the type of pressure you want with this particular button. You can switch from high to low pressure using this particular button.
- **Keep Warm/Cancel:** This allows you to cancel your cooking or keep your food warm.

Preset Buttons

Aside from the major cooking buttons, the Instant Pot also comes with present cooking buttons. The preset cooking buttons allow you to cook different types of food without having to worry which temperature settings will cook your food perfectly. In a nutshell, the preset button removes all the guesswork when cooking your food.

- **Meat/ Stew:** This button will cook meat like pork, beef, lamb, or veal at high temperature for 35 minutes.
- **Bean/Chili:** This button will cook all types of bean dishes at high temperature for 30 minutes.
- **Multigrain:** Cook different kinds of grains like barley, wheat, quinoa, and amaranth to name a few under high pressure. The preset cooking time is 20 minutes but you can adjust depending on your needs.
- **Porridge:** Cook rice porridge or even soups with this button. The preset cooking time is 20 minutes but you can adjust to as low as 15 minutes as long as you cook on high pressure.
- **Poultry:** Cook all types of poultry with this preset button. You can cook turkey, quail, chicken

and all types of game birds. Cook chicken dishes within the preset time of 35 minutes.

- **Rice:** Cook rice perfectly in Instant Pot. This particular button allows you to cook rice within 20 minutes. When cooking with rice, make sure that you do natural pressure release as rice tends to foam up and may block your Instant Pot's vents.
- **Soup:** This button allows you to cook soups of all kinds. It can cook soup at high pressure within 20 to 40 minutes.
- **Steam:** This particular button allows you to use the Instant Pot as a steamer so you can cook all kinds of steamed dishes.

Chapter 2: Pork, Beef, and Lamb Whole Food Instant Pot Recipes

Instant Pot Roast

Serves: 6
Preparation Time: 5
Cook Time: 1 hour

Ingredients

- 4 pounds chuck roast, cut into pieces
- 1 ½ cups beef broth
- 2 teaspoon fish sauce
- 2 tablespoons balsamic vinegar
- 2 parsnips, peeled
- 6 cloves of garlic, peeled
- 4 carrots, peeled and scrubbed
- Salt and pepper to taste

Instructions

1. Season beef with salt and pepper to taste.
2. Place inside the Instant Pot and add the rest of the ingredients.
3. Close the lid and make sure that the lid is securely closed.
4. After an hour, allow the Instant Pot to release the pressure naturally for at least 15 minutes.

5. Remove the meat from the Instant Pot and put in a plate. Allow to cool before slicing the beef.
6. Place all vegetables including the liquid in a blender and pulse until smooth.
7. Pour the sauce all over the beef slices.

Nutrition information: Calories per serving: 422; Carbohydrates: 11.76g; Protein: 81.8g; Fat: 25.77g; Sugar: 3.21g; Sodium: 654; Fiber: 1.4g

Beef and Plantain Curry

Serves: 6
Preparation Time: 15 minutes
Cook Time: 40 minutes

Ingredients

- 1 teaspoon ginger powder
- 1 teaspoon garlic powder
- 1 teaspoon turmeric powder
- 2 tablespoon coconut oil
- 1 teaspoon sea salt
- 3 tablespoon olive oil
- 2 onions, peeled and thinly sliced
- 2 pounds pot roast, cut into cubes
- 1 cup coconut milk
- 4 kaffir lime leaves
- 1 stick cinnamon
- 1 ripe plantain, sliced into chunks
- 1 tablespoon coriander leaves

Instructions

1. In a bowl, mix together the ginger powder, garlic powder, turmeric, coconut oil, and sea salt. Marinate the beef in the mixture for at least two hours in the fridge.

2. Press the sauté button on the Instant pot and heat olive oil. Add the onions and stir until translucent. Set aside.
3. Add the beef and brown on all sides. Set aside.
4. Pour the coconut oil in the pot and stir constantly to remove the browning at the bottom. Add the meat and onions back. Add the kaffir lime leaves and cinnamon stick.
5. Close the lid and make sure that the valve is set to "sealing".
6. Cook for 35 minutes using the manual setting.
7. Once the cooking time is completed, do quick pressure release.
8. Press the sauté function and add the plantain. Allow to simmer for 5 minutes without closing the lid.
9. Garnish with coriander leaves.

Nutrition information: Calories per serving: 442; Carbohydrates: 7.14g; Protein: 43.24g; Fat: 26.44g; Sugar: 2.62g; Sodium: 982mg; Fiber: 1.3g

Instant Pot Mexican Meatloaf

Serves: 6
Preparation Time: 10 minutes
Cook Time: 35 minutes

Ingredients

- 2 pounds grass-fed ground beef
- 1 cup chopped tomatoes
- 1 teaspoon cumin
- 1 teaspoon chili powder
- Teaspoon garlic powder
- 1 teaspoon onion powder
- 1 teaspoon paprika
- 1 teaspoon salt
- 1 teaspoon ground black pepper
- 1 pasture-laid egg
- 1 yellow onion, diced
- ¼ cup arrowroot starch
- 1 tablespoon ghee

Instructions

1. Mix all ingredients in a bowl except the ghee.
2. Use your hands to form a loaf with the mixture.
3. Press it firmly and coat the surface with oil
4. Wrap it in foil and place inside the Instant Pot lined with a steamer rack.
5. Pour a cup of water and close the lid.
6. Press the Meat button and cook for 35 minutes.

7. Do a quick release and take out the meatloaf.
8. Allow to cool before removing the foil wrap and slicing.

Nutrition information: Calories per serving: 393; Carbohydrates: 3.79g; Protein: 29.17g; Fat: 29.28g; Sugar: 1.26g; Sodium: 934mg; Fiber: 0.9g

Instant Pot Saucy Meatballs

Serves: 8
Preparation Time: 45 minutes
Cook Time: 35 minutes

Ingredients

- 1 ½ pounds of grass-fed ground beef
- ½ teaspoon salt
- ¼ teaspoon ground black pepper
- 4 tomatoes, chopped
- 1 cup organic tomato sauce
- 4 cloves of garlic, peeled and chopped
- 10 small bell peppers, chopped
- 1 onion, chopped
- ½ teaspoon garlic powder
- Salt and pepper to taste

Instructions

1. In a mixing bowl, combine the ground beef, salt and black pepper. Mix using your hands until well combined. Form meatballs using your hands and set aside in the fridge to set for at least 30 minutes.
2. Press the sauté button on the Instant Pot. Once hot, place the meatballs and sear the meatballs until all sides brown.

3. Pour the rest of the ingredients into the Instant Pot and close the lid.
4. Press the Meat button and cook for 35 minutes.
5. Serve.

Nutrition information: Calories per serving: 251; Carbohydrates: 11.93g; Protein: 17.53g; Fat: 15.78 g; Sugar: 6.54g; Sodium: 684mg; Fiber: 2.4g

Corned Beef and Cabbage

Serves: 6
Preparation Time: 5 minutes
Cook Time: 1 hour and 15 minutes

Ingredients

- 3 pounds corned beef brisket
- 3 cups beef broth
- 4 whole cloves
- 4 bay leaves
- ½ teaspoon mustard seeds
- 1 teaspoon white peppercorns
- 2 drops liquid smoke
- 1 head green cabbage, cut into chunks
- 4 Yukon gold potatoes, peeled and cut into chunks
- 4 carrots, peeled and cut into chunks
- Salt and pepper to taste

Instructions

1. Place the beef brisket in the Instant Pot and add the broth, cloves, bay leaves, mustard seeds, white peppercorns, and liquid smoke.
2. Close the lid and press the Meat button and cook for 55 minutes.
3. Once done, do natural pressure release.

4. Open the lid and add the vegetables. Press the sauté button and allow to cook the vegetables for 20 minutes. Season with salt and pepper to taste.

Nutrition information: Calories per serving: 734; Carbohydrates: 65.3g; Protein: 40.92g; Fat: 34.46g; Sugar:7.9 g; Sodium: 789mg; Fiber: 8.8 g

Instant Pot Pork and Pineapple Stew

Serves: 6
Preparation Time: 5 minutes
Cook Time: 45 minutes

Ingredients

- 2 pounds pork belly, cut into cubes
- 1 tablespoon coconut aminos
- ½ teaspoon sea salt
- ½ teaspoon ground cloves
- ½ teaspoon ground turmeric
- ½ teaspoon ginger powder
- 1 clove of garlic, chopped
- 1 onion, sliced
- 1 cup pineapple chunks
- 1 bay leaf
- 2 tablespoon organic fruit jam of your choice
- 1 cup bone broth

Instructions

1. Place all ingredients in the Instant Pot.
2. Close the lid and press the Meat button.
3. Cook for 45 minutes.
4. Do natural pressure release.
5. Serve warm.

Nutrition information: Calories per serving: 825; Carbohydrates:10.64 g; Protein: 14.4g; Fat: 80.12g; Sugar: 9.69g; Sodium: 1825mg; Fiber: 0.6g

Instant Pot Taco Meat

Serves: 6
Preparation Time: 5 minutes
Cook Time: 15 minutes

Ingredients

- 4 tablespoons oil
- 2 pounds grass-fed ground beef
- 2 onions, diced
- 5 cloves of garlic, minced
- 3 green bell peppers, deseeded and diced
- 2 teaspoons oregano
- 2 teaspoons chili powder
- 1 teaspoon dried basil
- 1 teaspoon salt
- ½ teaspoon ground black pepper
- ½ teaspoon turmeric powder
- 1 teaspoon cumin
- 1 teaspoon paprika
- ½ teaspoon cayenne pepper
- Cilantro, for garnishing

Instructions

1. Press the Sauté button on the Instant Pot and heat oil.
2. Add the ground beef, onions, and garlic. Sauté for three minutes.

3. Add all ingredients except for the cilantro and give a stir.
4. Close the lid and press the Meat button.
5. Cook for 10 minutes at high pressure.
6. Do natural pressure release.
7. Serve taco meat with cilantro.

Nutrition information: Calories per serving: 470; Carbohydrates: 8.08g; Protein: 28.22g; Fat: 36.87g; Sugar: 3.07g; Sodium: 735mg; Fiber: 1.8g

Jamaican Jerk Pork Roast

Serves: 12
Preparation Time: 2 hours
Cook Time: 1 hour

Ingredients

- 1 tablespoon olive oil
- 1 tablespoon garlic powder
- 2 teaspoons dried thyme
- 2 teaspoons dried parsley
- 1/4 teaspoon ground cinnamon
- 2 teaspoons onion powder
- 2 teaspoons sugar
- 2 teaspoons salt
- 1 teaspoon paprika
- 1/2 teaspoon black pepper
- 1/2 teaspoon dried crushed red pepper
- 1 teaspoon ground allspice
- 3 teaspoons cayenne pepper
- 1/2 teaspoon ground nutmeg
- 4 pounds pork shoulder, bone in
- ½ cup beef broth

Instructions

1. In a mixing bowl, combine the oil and the rest of the spices. This will be the dry rub.
2. Rub the pork shoulder with the rub and allow to marinade for at least 2 hours.

3. Place the pork shoulder in the Instant Pot and pour the broth.
4. Close the lid and press the Meat button.
5. Cook for 1 hour until the pork is very tender.
6. Do natural pressure release.

Nutrition information: Calories per serving: 427; Carbohydrates: 2.88g; Protein: 38.27; Fat:28.05 g; Sugar: 0.5g; Sodium: 835mg; Fiber: 0.5g

Instant Pot Mexican Beef

Serves: 6

Preparation Time: 10 minutes

Cook Time: 35 minutes

Ingredients

- 2 ½ pounds boneless beef brisket
- 1 tablespoon chili powder
- 1 ½ teaspoon salt
- 1 tablespoon grass-fed butter
- 1 onion, sliced
- 6 cloves of garlic, peeled and crushed
- 1 tablespoon organic tomato paste
- ½ cup roasted tomatoes
- ½ cup bone broth
- ½ teaspoon fish sauce
- A dash of ground pepper
- ½ cup cilantro for garnish

Instructions

1. In a mixing bowl, mix together the beef, chili powder, and salt. Set aside.
2. Press the sauté button on the Instant Pot and add the pork mixture and butter. Sauté for a few minutes until the meat has slightly browned.
3. Add the onion and garlic. Stir until the onions and garlic are translucent.

4. Pour in the tomato paste, tomatoes, broth, fish sauce and ground pepper.
5. Close the lid and press the Meat button.
6. Cook for 35 minutes.
7. Do natural pressure release and garnish with chopped cilantro.

Nutrition information: Calories per serving: 275; Carbohydrates: 5.4g; Protein: 41.88g; Fat: 10.04g; Sugar:2.51g; Sodium: 808mg; Fiber: 1.3g

Instant Pot Beef Stew

Serves: 8
Preparation Time: 15 minutes
Cook Time: 1 hour

Ingredients

- 3 tablespoons vegetable oil
- 2 ½ pounds chuck roast cut into chunks
- 1 teaspoon salt
- 1 cup chicken stock
- 1 cup tomato sauce
- teaspoon smoked paprika
- ½ teaspoon garlic powder
- 2 pounds potatoes, cut into chunks
- 8 ounces of carrots, cut into chunks
- 2 large onions, cut into chunks

Instructions

1. Press the sauté button on the Instant Pot.
2. Add the vegetable oil and the chuck roast chunks. Season with salt and allow to brown on all sides for 5 minutes.
3. Once the meat is brown, add the chicken stock and scrape the bottom of the pot to remove the browning.
4. Add the rest of the ingredients and close the lid.
5. Press the Meat button and cook for 55 minutes.

6. Do natural pressure release.

Nutrition information: Calories per serving: 367; Carbohydrates:34.56 g; Protein: 28.9g; Fat:15.3 g; Sugar: 12.5g; Sodium: 1034mg; Fiber: 9.2g

Sesame Garlic Beef Short Ribs

Serves: 6
Preparation Time: 5 minutes
Cook Time: 30 minutes

Ingredients

- 1-pound organic beef short ribs, bone removed and diced
- 2 tablespoon toasted sesame oil
- 2 tablespoon coconut aminos
- 2 cloves of garlic, minced
- 4 cremini mushrooms, chopped
- 2 scallions, minced
- Salt and pepper to taste
- Fresh lime wedges for garnish

Instructions

1. Place all ingredients except the fresh lime wedges in the Instant Pot.
2. Close the lid and press the Meat button.
3. Cook for 30 minutes.
4. Do natural pressure release and garnish with fresh lime wedges.

Nutrition information: Calories per serving: 171; Carbohydrates:2.21 g; Protein:15.6 g; Fat: 11.37g; Sugar:0.76 g; Sodium: 920 mg; Fiber:0.3 g

Hawaii Oxtail Soup

Serves: 4
Preparation Time: 5 minutes
Cook Time: 2 ½ hours

Ingredients

- 4 pounds oxtail
- 2 dried shiitake mushrooms
- 1-inch ginger, peeled and sliced
- 4 whole star anise
- Peel from ½ orange, chopped
- 1 teaspoon whole black peppercorns
- 4 cups chicken broth
- 1 teaspoon fish sauce
- Salt to taste

Instructions

1. Place all ingredients in the Instant Pot.
2. Close the lid and press the Meat button.
3. Cook for 2 ½ hours or until the oxtail is very soft.
4. Do natural pressure release.
5. Garnish with chopped green onions.

Nutrition information: Calories per serving: 782; Carbohydrates: 4.4g; Protein: 89.1g; Fat: 45.2g; Sugar: 1.2g; Sodium: 829mg; Fiber: 0.3g

Instant Pot Creole Pochero

Serves: 6
Preparation Time: 30 minutes
Cook Time: 1 hour

Ingredients

- 1 teaspoon paprika
- ½ teaspoon garlic powder
- ½ teaspoon onion powder
- ½ teaspoon dried thyme
- ½ teaspoon dried basil
- ½ teaspoon cayenne pepper
- 1 tablespoon grass-fed butter
- 3 pounds beef shank
- 1 onion, minced
- 1 garlic minced
- 2 tablespoon tomato paste
- 4 cups chicken broth
- 1 teaspoon apple cider vinegar
- 4 medium potatoes
- 3 carrots
- 3 stalks celery
- Salt and pepper to taste

Instructions

1. In a mixing bowl, combine the first 6 ingredients. This will be the Creole seasoning.

2. Place the beef shank in a large bowl and pour over the Creole seasoning. Set aside to marinate in the fridge for at least 30 minutes.
3. Press the Sauté button on the Instant pot and add the butter.
4. Add the beef and brown on all side for at least 3 minutes.
5. Add the onion and garlic and allow to cook until translucent
6. Pour the tomato paste and chicken broth. Scrape the bottom to remove the browning.
7. Add the rest of the ingredients.
8. Close the lid and press the Meat button and cook for 1 hour. Do natural pressure release.

Nutrition information: Calories per serving: 765; Carbohydrates: 51.6g; Protein:89.9 g; Fat: 20.25g; Sugar: 5.5g; Sodium: 921mg; Fiber: 7.3g

Pork Cheek Stew

Serves: 6
Preparation Time: 10 minutes
Cook Time: 40 minutes

Ingredients

- 2 tablespoon olive oil
- 4 pounds pork cheeks, patted dry and cut into strips
- 1 onion diced
- 6 cloves of garlic, chopped
- 1 ½ cups chicken broth
- 8 ounces cremini mushrooms
- 1 large leek, cut into chunks
- Juice from 1 ½ lemons, freshly squeezed
- Salt and pepper to taste

Instructions

1. Press the sauté button on the Instant Pot and add oil.
2. Add the patted pork cheeks, onions, and garlic. Sear the pork cheeks on all sides and make sure that the onions and garlic become translucent.
3. Add the rest of the ingredients and give a good swirl. Make sure that you scrape off the bottom to remove browning.
4. Close the lid and press the Meat button.
5. Cook for 40 minutes.

6. Allow to do natural pressure release.

Nutrition information: Calories per serving: 562; Carbohydrates: 20.2g; Protein:50.43 g; Fat: 21.4g; Sugar: 8.5g; Sodium: 701mg; Fiber: 8.7g

Instant Pot Spicy Beef Stew

Serves: 6
Preparation Time: 5 minutes
Cook Time: 45 minutes

Ingredients

- 2 tablespoon grass-fed butter
- 1-pound beef stew meat
- 1 onion, diced
- 3 medium potatoes, chopped
- 2 celery stalks, chopped
- 4 carrots, chopped
- 2 cups kale leaves
- 1 teaspoon garlic powder
- ½ teaspoon black pepper
- 2 cups bone broth
- Salt to taste

Instructions

1. Press the sauté button on the Instant Pot.
2. Add the butter and sauté the meat until all sides become brown.
3. Add the rest of the ingredients except for the salt.
4. Close the lid and set the Instant Pot to the Meat setting.
5. Cook for 45 minutes.
6. Do quick natural release and season with salt.

Nutrition information: Calories per serving: 492; Carbohydrates:10.2 g; Protein: 67.2g; Fat: 75.8g; Sugar: 3.2g; Sodium: 568mg; Fiber: 2.8g

Pork Roast with Cauliflower Gravy

Serves: 6
Preparation Time: 5 minutes
Cook Time: 1 hour and 30 minutes

Ingredients

- 4 cups cauliflower, chopped
- 1 onion, chopped
- 4 cloves of garlic, chopped
- 2 stalks of celery, chopped
- 2 cups water
- 3 pounds pork roast
- 1 teaspoon salt
- ½ teaspoon black pepper
- 8 ounces mushrooms

Instructions

1. In the bottom of the Instant Pot, place the cauliflower, onion, garlic, celery, and water.
2. Place the pork and mushrooms on top of the vegetables and season with salt and pepper.
3. Close the lid and press the Meat button. Cook for 90 minutes.
4. Do quick pressure release and remove the pork from the pressure cooker.
5. Place in a baking dish and bake in the oven for 10 minutes at 400°F.

6. Meanwhile, transfer the vegetables in the blender and pulse until smooth.
7. Serve the meat with the cauliflower gravy.

Nutrition information: Calories per serving: 498; Carbohydrates: 15.6g; Protein:45.2 g; Fat: 20.7g; Sugar: 2.6g; Sodium: 801mg; Fiber: 9.3g

Instant Pot Kalua Pork

Serves: 10
Preparation Time: 10 minutes
Cook Time: 1 hour and 40 minutes

Ingredients

- 5 pounds pork shoulder, bone in and cut into large chunks
- 1 tablespoon olive oil
- 1 teaspoon salt
- ½ cup diced pineapple
- 1 tablespoon liquid smoke
- 1 teaspoon fish sauce
- ½ cup water

Instructions

1. Press the sauté button on the Instant Pot.
2. Heat the olive oil and place the pork chunks. Season with salt. Sauté for a few minutes or until the pork pieces have turned golden brown.
3. Add the rest of the ingredients and scrape the bottom to remove the browning.
4. Close the lid and press the Meat button.
5. Cook for 1 hour and 40 minutes.
6. Do natural release.

Nutrition information: Calories per serving: 482; Carbohydrates:5.2 g; Protein: 89.2g; Fat: 73.3g; Sugar: 1.4g; Sodium: 923mg; Fiber:2.4 g

Pork Sirloin Tip Roast

Serves: 6
Preparation Time: 30 minutes
Cook Time: 1 hour

Ingredients

- ½ teaspoon black pepper
- ½ teaspoon salt
- ½ teaspoon garlic powder
- ½ teaspoon onion powder
- ¼ teaspoon chili powder
- 3 pounds pork sirloin tip roast
- 1 tablespoon vegetable oil
- 1 cup water
- ½ cup apple juice

Instructions

1. In a mixing bowl, combine the black pepper, salt, garlic powder, onion powder, and chili powder. This will be the dry rub mixture.
2. Rub the spice mixture onto the sirloin tip roast. Leave in the fridge to marinate for 30 minutes.
3. Press the sauté button and heat the vegetable oil.
4. Add the marinated sirloin into the pot and sear until all sides brown.
5. Add the water and apple juice. Scrape the bottom to remove the browning.

6. Close the lid and press the Meat button. Cook for 1 hour until the meat is very tender.
7. Do quick pressure release.

Nutrition information: Calories per serving: 523; Carbohydrates: 7.2g; Protein: 64.5g; Fat: 32.6g; Sugar: 1.2g; Sodium: 729mg; Fiber: 3.1g

Instant Pot Lechon Asado

Serves: 6
Preparation Time: 5 minutes
Cook Time: 30 minutes

Ingredients

- 6 pounds pork roast
- 8 cloves of garlic, minced
- 2/3 cup fresh orange juice, freshly squeezed
- 1/3 cup olive oil
- ½ teaspoon dried oregano
- ½ teaspoon cumin
- Salt and pepper to taste
- 1 onion, sliced

Instructions

1. Place all ingredients in a mixing bowl and mix together to coat the meat with the spices.
2. Allow to marinate in the fridge for at least 2 hours.
3. Press the sauté button in the Instant Pot and wait for it to warm.
4. Once warm, add the marinated beef and sauté until the sides turn brown.
5. Close the lid and press the Meat button.
6. Cook for 30 minutes until the meat is very tender.

Nutrition information: Calories per serving: 453; Carbohydrates: 15.3g; Protein:68.2 g; Fat:34.2 g; Sugar: 4g; Sodium: 672 mg; Fiber: 1.3g

Pork, Mung Bean and Rice Stew

Serves: 2
Preparation Time: 5 minutes
Cook Time: 30 minutes

Ingredients

- ½ cup mung beans
- ½ cup brown basmati rice
- ½ cup red onions, chopped
- 5 cloves of garlic
- 2 medium tomatoes
- 1-inch ginger, sliced
- ½ teaspoon cumin seeds
- ½ teaspoon turmeric
- 1 teaspoon ground coriander
- ½ teaspoon garam masala
- ¼ teaspoon cayenne pepper
- ½ teaspoon oil
- ½ pound ground pork
- 4 cups water
- 1 teaspoon lemon juice
- 1 ¼ teaspoon salt

Instructions

1. Soak the beans and rice in enough water. Set aside.

2. In a food processor, blend together the onions, garlic, tomato, ginger, and the rest of the spices. Add oil.
3. Press the sauté button on the Instant Pot and add the pureed spice mix.
4. Continue stirring until the spices are fragrant. Stir in the pork.
5. Add the water, rice and mung beans.
6. Season with lemon juice, salt and pepper.
7. Close the lid and press the Manual button.
8. Cook for 30 minutes.
9. Do natural pressure release.

Nutrition information: Calories per serving: 432; Carbohydrates: 28.2g; Protein: 25.3g; Fat: 10.2g; Sugar: 5.4g; Sodium: 341mg; Fiber: 15.2g

Chapter 3: Seafood Whole Food Instant Pot Recipes

Old Bay Fish Tacos

Serves: 8
Preparation Time: 10 minutes
Cook Time: 3 minutes

Ingredients
- 2 large cod fillets
- 1 tablespoon organic Old Bay seasoning
- 2 tablespoons olive oil
- 8 corn tortillas
- 1 ripe medium tomatoes, diced
- 2 tablespoon fresh cilantro, chopped
- ½ medium white onion, diced
- Juice from 1 lime, freshly squeezed
- ½ cup quesadilla cheese

Instructions
1. Place a cup of water in the Instant Pot and place a steamer rack.
2. Season fish fillets with Old Bay seasoning and place in the steamer rack.
3. Close the lid and press the Steam button. Cook for 3 minutes. Do natural pressure release.

4. Meanwhile, fry the tortillas in a skillet on medium high heat until crispy. Set aside.
5. Prepare the taco toppings by mixing the remaining ingredients.
6. Assemble the taco by placing the steamed fish inside the taco and top with the vegetables and cheese.

Nutrition information: Calories per serving: 323; Carbohydrates: 15g; Protein: 21g; Fat: 28g; Sugar: 6 g; Sodium: 891mg; Fiber: 2.3g

Instant Pot Tomato Tuna Pasta and Capers

Serves: 6

Preparation Time: 5 minutes

Cook Time: 10 minutes

Ingredients

- 2 tablespoons olive oil
- 2 cloves of garlic, chopped
- 2 cups organic pasta
- 1-pound tuna, sliced into strips
- 1 can diced tomatoes
- 1 teaspoon oregano
- ½ teaspoon dried chilies
- ½ cup red wine
- Salt and pepper to taste
- 2 tablespoons capers
- Grated parmesan cheese for garnish

Instructions

1. Press the sauté button on the Instant Pot.
2. Add the oil and sauté the garlic for a few minutes until fragrant.
3. Add the pasta, tuna slices, tomatoes, oregano, and dried chilies.
4. Stir in the red wine and season with salt and pepper to taste.

5. Close the lid and press the Manual button. Adjust the cooking time to 8 minutes.
6. Do natural pressure release.
7. Once the lid is open, stir in capers and top with parmesan cheese.

Nutrition information: Calories per serving: 150; Carbohydrates: 6.9g; Protein: 15.96g; Fat: 6.39g; Sugar: 4.24g; Sodium: 78mg; Fiber: 2.3g

Instant Pot Seafood Boil

Serves: 6
Preparation Time: 5 minutes
Cook Time: 6 minutes

Ingredients

- 3 cups red potatoes, cleaned and halved
- 6-pieces corn on the cob
- 6 fennel sausages
- 1 ½ pounds snow crabs, cleaned
- 1 ½ pounds large shrimps, cleaned and rinsed
- 3 cups water
- 1 tablespoon salt
- 1 tablespoon paprika
- 1 bay leaf
- 3 sage leaves
- 1 bulb of garlic, crushed

Instructions

1. Place all ingredients in the Instant Pot.
2. Close the lid and press the Manual button.
3. Cook for 6 minutes.
4. Do quick pressure release and remove the seafood from the pot to avoid overcooking.

Nutrition information: Calories per serving: 235; Carbohydrates: 13.61g; Protein: 37.49g; Fat: 2.62g; Sugar: 1.08g; Sodium: 167mg; Fiber:1.7 g

Japanese Seafood Curry

Serves: 4
Preparation Time: 20 minutes
Cook Time: 15 minutes

Ingredients

- 3 cups water
- 1 2"x3" dried kelp or kombu
- 1 tablespoon vegetable oil
- 3 onions, sliced
- 2 cloves of garlic, minced
- 1-inch ginger, grated
- 6 ounces shrimps, shelled and deveined
- 12 medium-sized clams or mussels, soaked in salted water overnight
- 6 ounces bay scallops
- 6 ounces calamari or sliced squid
- ¼ cup white wine
- 6 mushrooms, sliced
- 1 pack Japanese curry roux
- 1 tablespoon soy sauce
- ¼ apple, cored and grated

Instructions

1. Make the dashi stock by mixing the water and kombu an hour before cooking.
2. Press the sauté button on the Instant Pot and heat the vegetable oil.

3. Sauté onions, garlic, and ginger until fragrant.
4. Stir in the shrimps, clams, scallops, and calamari. Pour in the white wine and continue stirring for another minute.
5. Add the prepared dashi stock and mushrooms. Stir in the curry roux and soy sauce.
6. Close the lid and press the manual button. Cook for 5 minutes.
7. Do quick pressure release and add the grated apples while still hot.
8. Serve over warm white rice.

Nutrition information: Calories per serving: 204; Carbohydrates: 7.44g; Protein: 27.02g; Fat: 7.43g; Sugar: 3.32g; Sodium: 532mg; Fiber: 0.6g

Instant Pot Asian Salmon

Serves: 2
Preparation Time: 2 hours
Cook Time: 13 minutes

Ingredients

- ¼ cup water
- ½ cup soy sauce
- ¼ cup mirin
- 1 tablespoon sesame oil
- 1 clove of garlic, minced
- 1 tablespoon ginger, grated
- 2 tablespoons brown sugar
- 2 thick salmon fillets
- 2 teaspoons sesame seeds
- 3 chopped green onions, for garnish

Instructions

1. In a small bowl, mix together the water, soy sauce, mirin, and sesame oil. Add in the garlic, ginger and brown sugar.
2. Pour over salmon fillets and allow to marinate for at least 2 hours in the fridge.
3. Place the entire salmon including the marinade in the Instant Pot.
4. Close the lid and press the manual button. Cook for 3 minutes.

5. Do natural pressure release and remove the salmon fillet from the Instant Pot.
6. Press the sauté button and allow the sauce to thicken for at least 10 minutes.
7. Pour sauce over salmon and garnish with sesame seeds and green onions.

Nutrition information: Calories per serving: 296; Carbohydrates:23.31 g; Protein: 6.28g; Fat: 20.52g; Sugar: 16.53g; Sodium: 523mg; Fiber: 3.6g

Fish with Orange and Ginger Sauce

Serves: 4
Preparation Time: 10 minutes
Cook Time: 7 minutes

Ingredients

- Olive oil
- 4 fish fillets, patted dry
- Salt and pepper to taste
- Juice from 1 orange, freshly squeezed
- Zest from 1 orange, grated
- 1 thumb-size ginger, grated
- 1 cup fish stock
- 4 spring onions, chopped

Instructions

1. Rub oil on the fish fillets then season with salt and pepper to taste.
2. In the Instant Pot, pour orange juice, orange zest, ginger, and fish stock.
3. Place a steamer basket on top of the liquid and place the fish gently.
4. Close the lid and press the Steam button.
5. Cook for 7 minutes.
6. Do quick pressure release and garnish with chopped spring onions.
7. Discard the liquid.

Nutrition information: Calories per serving: 430; Carbohydrates: 27.61g; Protein: 15.6g; Fat: 11.71g; Sugar:8.92g; Sodium: 645mg; Fiber: 1g

Instant Pot Thai Fish

Serves: 2
Preparation Time: 10 minutes
Cook Time: 10 minutes

Ingredients

- 1 cup coconut milk
- 1 sprig Thai basil
- 1 sprig coriander
- 1 tablespoon cayenne pepper
- 1 tablespoon fish sauce
- Zest from 1 lime
- Juice from ½ lime, freshly squeezed
- 2 teaspoons brown sugar
- 1 teaspoon garlic, minced
- 1 tablespoon fresh ginger
- 2 fish fillets

Instructions

1. In a blender, mix together coconut milk, Thai basil, coriander, cayenne pepper, fish sauce, lime zest, lime juice, brown sugar, garlic, and ginger.
2. Pulse until it forms a smooth paste.
3. Arrange the fish fillets in the Instant Pot and pour over sauce.
4. Close the lid and select the Manual button.
5. Cook for 10 minutes.

6. Do quick pressure release.

Nutrition information: Calories per serving: 529; Carbohydrates: 32.3g; Protein: 17.1; Fat: 40.31; Sugar: 9.7g; Sodium: 742mg; Fiber: 4.1g

Green Chili Mahi Mahi

Serves: 6

Preparation Time: 5 minutes

Cook Time: 5 minutes

Ingredients

- ¼ cup canola oil
- 3 tablespoons chili powder
- 1 can organic tomato sauce
- 2 teaspoons ground cumin
- 1 cup chicken broth
- 1 tablespoon garlic, chopped
- ½ teaspoon onion powder
- 6 Mahi Mahi fillets, thawed
- Salt and pepper to taste
- 2 tablespoons butter

Instructions

1. Mix in a bowl, the canola oil, chili powder, tomato sauce, ground cumin, broth, garlic and onion powder.
2. Arrange the fish fillets in the Instant Pot and pour over sauce. Season with salt and pepper to taste.
3. Close the lid and press the Manual seasoning.
4. Cook for 5 minutes.
5. Do quick pressure release and add the butter while still warm.

Nutrition information: Calories per serving: 444; Carbohydrates: 11.59g; Protein: 29.16g; Fat: 31.75g; Sugar:1.4 g; Sodium: 871mg; Fiber: 6.7g

Instant Pot Lemon and Dill Fish Packets

Serves: 2

Preparation Time: 10 minutes

Cook Time: 6 minutes

Ingredients

- 2 fish fillets
- Salt and pepper to taste
- 1 teaspoon garlic powder
- 2 sprigs of fresh dill
- 4 slices of lemon
- 2 tablespoons butter

Instructions

1. Place a steam rack in the Instant Pot and pour 1 cup of water
2. Cut 2 large squares of parchment paper.
3. Place a fillet in the middle of the parchment paper.
4. Season the fillet with salt, pepper, and garlic powder.
5. Place a generous amount of fresh dill, lemon and a tablespoon of butter on each fillet.
6. Close the parchment paper and seal off the edges.
7. Place on the steam rack.
8. Close the lid and press the Steam button.
9. Cook for 6 minutes.
10. Allow to release the pressure naturally.

Nutrition information: Calories per serving: 348; Carbohydrates: 25.53g; Protein: 14.51g; Fat: 22.99g; Sugar:3.6 g; Sodium: 478mg; Fiber: 1.2g

Sweet and Spicy Mahi Mahi

Serves: 2
Preparation Time: 2 hours
Cook Time: 5 minutes

Ingredients

- 2 Mahi Mahi fillets
- Salt and pepper to taste
- 1 clove of garlic, minced
- 1-inch piece ginger, grated
- Juice from ½ lime, freshly squeezed
- 2 tablespoons honey
- 1 tablespoon soy sauce

Instructions

1. Season the fish with salt and pepper. Set aside.
2. In a bowl combine the garlic, ginger, lime juice, honey, and soy sauce. Give a good whisk. Pour over the fish fillet and allow to marinate for 2 hours.
3. Pour a cup of water in the Instant Pot and place a steam rack at the bottom of the Instant Pot.
4. Place the fish fillets on the rack and pour over the sauce.
5. Close the lid and press the Steam button.
6. Cook for 5 minutes.
7. Do natural pressure release.

Nutrition information: Calories per serving: 347; Carbohydrates: 30.49g; Protein: 20.78g; Fat:16.9 g; Sugar: 15.2g; Sodium: 1933mg; Fiber:5.8 g

Instant Pot Sardines in Oil

Serves: 12
Preparation Time: 10 minutes
Cook Time: 1 hour

Ingredients

- 1-pound sardines, gutted and heads removed
- 3 cups corn oil
- 1 cup pickled cucumbers, drained
- 1 tablespoon salt
- ½ teaspoon ground black pepper
- 3 dried chilies
- 1 bay leaf
- 1 large carrot, peeled and sliced

Instructions

1. Place all ingredients in the Instant Pot.
2. Close the lid and press the Manual button.
3. Cook on high for an hour or until the bones are also soft.
4. Do natural pressure release.

Nutrition information: Calories per serving: 576; Carbohydrates: 0.42g; Protein: 9.4g; Fat: 60.35g; Sugar: 0g; Sodium: 896mg; Fiber:0g

Instant Pot Seafood Gumbo

Serves: 8

Preparation Time: 10 minutes

Cook Time: 30 minutes

Ingredients

- 2 tablespoon olive oil
- 1 onion, chopped
- 2 tablespoons minced garlic
- 2 red bell peppers, chopped
- 2 smoked sausages, chopped
- 3 celery stalks, chopped
- 6 cups fish stock
- 1-pound tiger prawns, shelled and deveined
- 1-pound crabmeat
- 24 oysters, shucked
- 2 tablespoon dried thyme
- Salt and pepper to taste
- ½ cup all-purpose flour
- ¼ cup oil
- 8 cups cooked rice
- ½ cup green onions, chopped
- Parsley for garnish

Instructions

1. In the Instant Pot, press the sauté button and add oil. Sauté the onions and garlic until translucent before stirring in red bell peppers, smoked

sausages and celery stalks. Stir in the fish stock, tiger prawns, crabmeat, and oysters. Season with thyme, salt and pepper.

2. Close the lid and press the Manual button. Cook for 10 minutes.

3. Meanwhile, heat the ¼ cup oil in a skillet and stir in the flour until it turns into slightly golden in color. Set aside.

4. Once the Instant Pot sets off, do quick pressure release. Ladle some of the soup from the Instant Pot into the roux and whisk to create a smooth paste. Pour back into the Instant Pot and cook for another 10 minutes. Stir in rice and garnish with green onions and parsley.

Nutrition information: Calories per serving:807; Carbohydrates: 104.7g; Protein: 24.8g; Fat:48.74 g; Sugar: 3.66g; Sodium:1934 mg; Fiber: 29.6g

Steamed Fish Patra Ni Maachi

Serves: 6
Preparation Time: 5 minutes
Cook Time: 10 minutes

Ingredients

- 2 cups coriander leaves
- 2 green chilies
- ½ ginger
- ½ teaspoon lime juice
- ½ teaspoon cumin powder
- ½ teaspoon chaat masala
- ½ teaspoon salt
- 2 teaspoons water
- 1-pound tilapia fillets
- 1 ½ cup water

Instructions

1. Place in a food processor or blender the coriander leaves, chilies, ginger, lime juice, cumin powder, chaat masala, salt and water. Pulse until you form a smooth paste. This will be your green chutney.
2. Place the tilapia fillets in the Instant Pot.
3. Pour over the green chutney and add the water.
4. Close the lid and press the manual button.
5. Cook for 10 minutes.

Nutrition information: Calories per serving: 134; Carbohydrates: 1g; Protein: 22g; Fat: 3g; Sugar: 0g; Sodium: 515mg; Fiber: 0.8g

Instant Pot Mok Pa

Serves: 6
Preparation Time: 15 minutes
Cook Time: 10 minutes

Ingredients

- 2 pounds white fish, cut into 2-inch strips
- 3 tablespoon sticky rice, soaked overnight then drained
- 1 stalk lemon grass
- 1 shallot, chopped
- 2 cloves of garlic, peeled
- 5 Thai bird chilies
- 2 tablespoons water
- ½ cup cilantro leaves
- 1 cup fresh dill, chopped
- 12 kaffir lime leaves
- 2 tablespoons fish sauce
- 1 tablespoon green onions, chopped
- 2 cups eggplants, sliced
- 1 banana leaf

Instructions

1. Place fish in a bowl. Set aside.
2. In a food processor, pulse the rice, lemon grass, shallot, garlic, and Thai bird chilies to form a paste. You can also do this in a mortar and pestle. Dilute with water.

3. Pour the mixture into the fish and add cilantro and dill. Stir in the kaffir leaves, fish sauce and green onions.
4. Take an aluminum foil and line a banana leaf on top. Arrange the fish and eggplants before folding the foil to create a small packet with fish and vegetables.
5. Pour water in the Instant Pot and place a steamer rack. Place the aluminum packets on the steam rack. Close the lid and press the Steam button. Cook for 10 minutes.
6. Do quick pressure release.

Nutrition information: Calories per serving: 325; Carbohydrates: 15.2g; Protein:24.5g; Fat: 18.3g; Sugar: 3.4g; Sodium: 893mg; Fiber: 7.4g

Squid in Coconut Milk Curry

Serves: 4

Preparation Time: 5 minutes

Cook Time: 15 minutes

Ingredients

- 1 tablespoon olive oil
- 3 cloves of garlic, minced
- 1 onion, chopped
- ½ pound squid rings
- ½ red bell pepper, chopped
- 1 tomato, chopped
- 1 can coconut milk
- 4 tablespoons curry powder

Instructions

1. Press the sauté button on the Instant Pot.
2. Add olive oil and sauté the garlic and onions until fragrant and translucent.
3. Add the red bell pepper, tomatoes, and squid.
4. Stir in the coconut milk and curry powder.
5. Season with salt and pepper if needed.
6. Close the lid and press the Manual button.
7. Cook for 15 minutes.

Nutrition information: Calories per serving: 125; Carbohydrates: 10.3g; Protein: 10.56g; Fat:5.15 g; Sugar: 2.46g; Sodium: 562mg; Fiber: 4.3g

Instant Pot Fish Chowder

Serves: 4
Preparation Time: 10 minutes
Cook Time: 10 minutes

Ingredients

- 2 tablespoons butter
- 1 onion, chopped
- 3 stalks of celery, chopped
- 1 large carrot, chopped
- 1-pound potatoes, scrubbed and diced
- 1-pound white fish, cut into 1 ½ inch chunks
- 2 cups fish stock
- 1 cup cold water
- 1 bay leaf
- ½ teaspoon dried thyme
- 1 cup frozen corn
- ½ cups milk
- Salt and pepper to taste
- ¼ cup fresh parsley, chopped

Instructions

1. Press the sauté button on the Instant Pot and heat the butter. Sauté the onions until translucent.
2. Stir in the celery, carrots, and potatoes for a minute. Add in the fish, stock, water, bay leaf, dried thyme, and corn.
3. Close the lid and press the Manual button.

4. Cook for 4 minutes.
5. Do quick pressure release to open the lid.
6. While the lid isn't in place, press the sauté button and add the milk. Season with salt and pepper. Allow to cook for 5 minutes.
7. Garnish with parsley.

Nutrition information: Calories per serving: 352; Carbohydrates: 36.39g; Protein: 27.13g; Fat:11.08 g; Sugar:6.41 g; Sodium:699 mg; Fiber: 4.9g

Steamed Shrimp in Coconut Milk

Serves: 4

Preparation Time: 10 minutes

Cook Time: 10 minutes

Ingredients

- 1-pound shrimp, shelled and deveined
- 1 tablespoon minced ginger
- 1 tablespoon minced garlic
- ½ teaspoon turmeric
- 1 teaspoon salt
- ½ teaspoon cayenne pepper
- 1 teaspoon garam masala
- ½ can coconut milk

Instructions

1. Pour a cup of water in the Instant Pot. Place a steam rack at the bottom.
2. In a heat-resistant that will fit inside the Instant Pot, mix together the shrimp and all the ingredients. Cover the pot with foil.
3. Place on the steam rack.
4. Close the lid and press the Steam button.
5. Cook for 3 minutes.
6. Do natural pressure release.

Nutrition information: Calories per serving: 236; Carbohydrates: 4g; Protein: 24g; Fat: 13g; Sugar: 1g; Sodium: 1470mg; Fiber: 1g

Cajun Shrimps with Cheese

Serves: 5
Preparation Time: 5 minutes
Cook Time: 4 minutes

Ingredients

- 1 tablespoon unsalted butter
- ¼ red bell pepper, chopped
- ¼ green bell pepper, chopped
- 30 tiger prawns, shelled and deveined
- 1 tablespoon Cajun spice
- ¾ cup cheddar cheese, shredded
- 2/3 cup milk

Instructions

1. Press the sauté button on the Instant Pot and wait until it is hot.
2. Melt the butter and sauté the bell peppers.
3. Stir in the prawns and Cajun spice.
4. Sprinkle on top the cheese and pour milk.
5. Close the lid and press the Manual button.
6. Cook for 4 minutes.
7. Do natural pressure release.

Nutrition information: Calories per serving: 342; Carbohydrates: 10.4g; Protein: 26.5g; Fat: 40.7g; Sugar: 2.3g; Sodium: 944mg; Fiber: 3.2g

Tuna Noodle Casserole

Serves: 4
Preparation Time: 5 minutes
Cook Time: 10 minutes

Ingredients

- 2 tablespoons butter
- ¼ cup onion, diced
- 2 stalks celery, diced
- 2 carrots, peeled and chopped
- 1 cup mushroom, chopped finely
- 4 cups tuna, chopped
- 1 cup frozen peas
- 1 ½ cups hot water
- 12 ounces egg noodles, uncooked
- Salt and pepper to taste
- cup milk
- 1 cup cheddar cheese, shredded

Instructions

1. Press the sauté button on the Instant Pot.
2. Melt the butter and sauté the onions, celery and carrots. Stir in the mushrooms and continue stirring until wilted.
3. Add the tuna and frozen peas. Stir in until the tuna meat is seared.
4. Pour in the hot water and egg noodles.
5. Stir in the milk and top with cheddar cheese.

6. Close the lid and press the Manual button.
7. Cook for 4 minutes

Nutrition information: Calories per serving: 380; Carbohydrates: 32.6g; Protein: 38.18g; Fat: 11.3g; Sugar: 6.34g; Sodium: 657mg; Fiber: 1.7g

Lemon Pepper Salmon

Serves: 4
Preparation Time: 5 minutes
Cook Time: 10 minutes

Ingredients

- ¾ cup water
- A sprig of parsley, chopped
- A sprig of basil
- 1-pound salmon fillet, with skin on
- 3 teaspoons butter
- ¼ teaspoon salt
- ½ teaspoon black pepper
- ½ lemon, thinly sliced
- 1 zucchini, julienned
- 1 red bell pepper, julienned
- 1 carrot, julienned

Instructions

1. Pour water in the Instant Pot. Stir in the parsley and basil. Place a steam rack at the bottom of the pot.
2. Place the salmon skin down on the rack and season with butter, salt and pepper. Place the lemon slices on top.
3. Close the lid and press the Steam button for 10 minutes.
4. Do natural pressure release.

5. Serve on bed of julienned zucchini, red pepper, and carrot.

Nutrition information: Calories per serving: 276; Carbohydrates: 3.28g; Protein: 26.66g; Fat: 17g; Sugar: 1.45g; Sodium:325 mg; Fiber: 0.7g

Chapter 4: Chicken Whole Food Instant Pot Recipes

Whole Roasted Rosemary Chicken

Serves: 8

Preparation Time: 20 minutes

Cook Time: 1 hour

Ingredients

- 1 whole chicken, innards removed and patted dry
- 1 tablespoon fresh rosemary, chopped
- 1 ½ tablespoons olive oil
- 6 cloves of garlic, minced
- ½ teaspoon paprika
- 1 teaspoon salt
- ¼ teaspoon black pepper
- Zest from 1 lemon, grated
- 1 cup chicken broth
- 1 large onion, quartered

Instructions

1. Press the sauté button on the Instant Pot.
2. While it is heating up, make the spice rub my mixing the rosemary, olive oil, garlic, paprika, salt, and pepper. Stir in the lemon zest.
3. Rub the chicken with the spice mixture and massage until all sides are covered.

4. Drizzle olive oil in the pan and place the chicken breast side down. Leave for 4 minutes before flipping the chicken on the other side.
5. Remove the chicken and pour in the chicken broth. Scrape the bottom to remove the browning.
6. Add the onions.
7. Place the chicken breast-side down again.
8. Close the lid and press the Poultry button and cook for 1 hour.
9. Do quick pressure release.

Nutrition information: Calories per serving:325; Carbohydrates: 2.91g; Protein: 27.96g; Fat: 21g; Sugar: 0.8g; Sodium: 365mg; Fiber:0.5 g

Root Beer Chicken Wings

Serves: 12
Preparation Time: 5 minutes
Cook Time: 45 minutes

Ingredients

- 5 pounds chicken wings
- 1 can organic root beer
- ¼ cup brown sugar

Instructions

1. Place all ingredients in the Instant Pot.
2. Close the lid and press the Poultry button.
3. Cook for 45 minutes.

Nutrition information: Calories per serving: 326; Carbohydrates: 21.65g; Protein:45.9 g; Fat:14.3 g; Sugar: 15g; Sodium: 872mg; Fiber: 0.8g

Seasoned Instant Pot Chicken

Serves: 8
Preparation Time: 10 minutes
Cook Time: 1 hour and 15 minutes

Ingredients

- 1 whole chicken
- Salt and pepper to taste
- 2 tablespoons olive oil
- 1 ½ cups chicken broth

Instructions

1. Season the chicken with salt and pepper.
2. Press the sauté button on the Instant Pot and heat oil.
3. Brown the chicken on all sides. Once the chicken is browned on all sides, remove it from the Instant Pot.
4. Pour the chicken broth and scrape the bottom to remove the browning.
5. Place the chicken back in the Instant Pot.
6. Close the lid and press the Poultry button.
7. Cook for 1 hour.
8. Do natural pressure release.

Nutrition information: Calories per serving: 463; Carbohydrates: 2g; Protein: 68.4g; Fat: 23.1g; Sugar: 0g; Sodium: 346mg; Fiber: 0g

Instant Pot Whole Soy Chicken

Serves: 12

Preparation Time: 10 minutes

Cook Time: 1 hour

Ingredients

- 2 pounds whole chicken
- Salt and pepper
- 1 tablespoon olive oil
- 5 carrots, cut into chunks
- 1 cup trimmed beans, washed
- 1 cup mushrooms, washed
- 1 onion, peeled and chopped
- 1 ½ lime, zested and juiced
- 1 tablespoon fish sauce
- 1 tablespoon soy sauce
- 2 tablespoons rice wine
- A handful of coriander for garnish
- 2 cups water

Instructions

1. Season the chicken with salt and pepper.
2. Press the sauté button on the Instant Pot and heat the oil. Place the chicken and allow to sear on all sides.
3. Remove the chicken from the Instant Pot and pour the rest of the ingredients.
4. Scrape the bottom to remove the browning.

5. Place the chicken back.
6. Close the lid and press the Poultry button.
7. Cook for 1 hour.
8. Do natural pressure release.

Nutrition information: Calories per serving: 194; Carbohydrates: 20.78g; Protein: 13.37g; Fat:7.09 g; Sugar: 5.23g; Sodium: 673mg; Fiber:3.8 g

Thrice-Cooked Tequila Lime Chicken

Serves: 6
Preparation Time: 15 minutes
Cook Time: 45 minutes

Ingredients

- 1 cup water
- 2 pounds chicken breasts
- ½ teaspoon coriander powder
- ½ teaspoon cumin power
- ½ teaspoon chili flakes
- ½ teaspoon garlic powder
- Salt and pepper to taste
- ½ cup tequila
- Zest of 1 lime, grated
- 1/3 cup lime juice, freshly squeezed
- 2 tablespoons brown sugar

Instructions

1. Put a cup of water in the Instant Pot and place a steam rack at the bottom.
2. Arrange the chicken pieces on the steam rack.
3. Cook for 10 minutes. Allow to release the pressure naturally.
4. Meanwhile, make the marinade by combining the remaining ingredients in a bowl.
5. Once you can open the lid, transfer the chicken in a baking pan lined with parchment paper. Brush

the chicken pieces with the marinade and bake for 15 minutes at 400°F.

6. When the wings are crispy, dump them in a saucepan with the marinade and toss to coat at medium flame.

Nutrition information: Calories per serving: 280; Carbohydrates: 4.84 g; Protein: 31.28g; Fat: 14.09g; Sugar: 2.09g; Sodium:536 mg; Fiber: 0.3g

Sweet and Sour Chicken Wings

Serves: 6
Preparation Time: 10 minutes
Cook Time: 1 hour and 5 minutes

Ingredients

- 1 pound's chicken wings
- ½ tablespoon soy sauce
- ¼ cup brown sugar
- ¼ cup organic tomato ketchup
- Salt and pepper to taste

Instructions

1. Place all ingredients in the Instant Pot.
2. Give a good stir to coat the chicken pieces.
3. Close the lid and press the Poultry button.
4. Cook for 45 minutes.
5. Do natural pressure release.
6. Place in a baking pan and bake for 10 minutes for 400°F or until the skin is crispy.

Nutrition information: Calories per serving: 138; Carbohydrates: 10.27g; Protein: 16.92g; Fat: 2.94g; Sugar: 8g; Sodium: 492mg; Fiber: 0.9g

Honey Garlic Chicken

Serves: 6

Preparation Time: 5 minutes

Cook Time: 20 minutes

Ingredients

- 1 ½ pounds chicken breasts, cut into cubes
- 2 green onions, sliced
- 6 tablespoons honey
- 1 teaspoon onion powder
- 3 cloves of garlic, minced
- ½ teaspoon garlic powder
- 1 ½ tablespoon soy sauce
- ½ tablespoon sriracha sauce
- 3 teaspoons cornstarch + 2 tablespoons water

Instructions

1. Place all ingredients in the Instant Pot except the cornstarch and water mixture.
2. Give a stir and close the lid.
3. Press the poultry button and cook for 15 minutes.
4. Do quick natural release.
5. Press the sauté button and stir in the cornstarch slurry.
6. Cook for another 5 minutes until the sauce thickens.

Nutrition information: Calories per serving: 275; Carbohydrates: 19.4g; Protein: 24.2g; Fat: 11.23g; Sugar:16.2 g; Sodium: 871mg; Fiber: 0.6g

Instant Pot Chicken Curry

Serves: 6
Preparation Time: 5 minutes
Cook Time: 15 minutes

Ingredients

- 1 tablespoon olive oil
- 2 tablespoons curry powder
- 1 large onion, chopped
- 4 cloves of garlic, minced
- 1 thumb-size ginger, grated
- 2 cups tomatoes, chopped
- Salt and pepper to taste
- 1 can light coconut milk
- 1 tablespoon sugar
- 2 pounds boneless chicken breasts, cubed

Instructions

1. Press the sauté button on the Instant Pot and add oil. Once the oil is hot, add the curry powder and stir for 45 seconds. Add in the onion, garlic, and ginger and cook for another minute.
2. Stir in the tomatoes and season with salt and pepper to taste.
3. Add in the rest of the ingredients.
4. Close the lid and press the Poultry button.
5. Adjust the cooking time to 12 minutes.
6. Do natural pressure release.

7. Serve with rice.

Nutrition information: Calories per serving: 238; Carbohydrates: 8.21g; Protein:35.5 g; Fat: 6.6g; Sugar: 4g; Sodium: 722mg; Fiber: 2.2g

Instant Pot Salsa Chicken

Serves: 3
Preparation Time: 5 minutes
Cook Time: 15 minutes

Ingredients

- 3 tablespoons coconut oil
- ¾ cup chopped onion
- 3 chicken breasts
- Salt and pepper to taste
- 1 cup water
- 1 cup organic salsa
- 1 tablespoon coconut aminos
- 1 teaspoon hot sauce
- ½ teaspoon fish sauce

Instructions

1. Press the sauté button on the Instant Pot and add coconut oil.
2. Sauté the onion until translucent. Stir in the chicken breasts and season with salt and pepper to taste.
3. Pour in the water, salsa, aminos, hot sauce, and fish sauce.
4. Close the lid and choose the Poultry button.
5. Cook for 15 minutes.

Nutrition information: Calories per serving: 660; Carbohydrates: 10.2g; Protein: 62.5g; Fat: 40.6g; Sugar: 5.6g; Sodium: 1647mg; Fiber: 2.3g

Instant Pot Mango Pineapple Chicken

Serves: 4
Preparation Time: 10 minutes
Cook Time: 10 minutes

Ingredients

- 3 chicken breasts, sliced
- ½ cup pineapple, sliced
- 1 ripe mango, cubed
- 1 sprig cilantro
- Salt and pepper to taste

Instructions

1. Place all ingredients in the Instant Pot.
2. Close the lid and press the Poultry button.
3. Cook for 10 minutes.
4. Do natural pressure release.

Nutrition information: Calories per serving: 397; Carbohydrates: 5.97g; Protein: 45.7g; Fat: 20.3g; Sugar: 3.1g; Sodium: 494mg; Fiber: 1.3g

Instant Pot Balsamic Chicken

Serves: 6
Preparation Time: 5 minutes
Cook Time: 15 minutes

Ingredients

- 2 pounds chicken breasts, bones removed
- 1 cup tomatoes, chopped
- 1 red onion, sliced
- 2 cloves of garlic, minced
- ½ cup balsamic vinegar
- ½ teaspoon each garlic powder, basil, and oregano
- Salt and pepper to taste

Instructions

1. Place all ingredients in the Instant Pot.
2. Give a good stir.
3. Close the lid and press the Poultry button.
4. Cook for 15 minutes.

Nutrition information: Calories per serving: 289; Carbohydrates: 5.96g; Protein: 32.2g; Fat: 14.1g; Sugar: 1.3g; Sodium: 824mg; Fiber: 2.5g

Thai Yellow Chicken Curry

Serves: 8

Preparation Time: 10 minutes

Cook Time: 20 minutes

Ingredients

- 1 tablespoon vegetable oil
- 1 onion, sliced
- 3 cloves of garlic, crushed
- ½ inch piece of ginger, crushed
- 4 tablespoons yellow curry paste
- 2 red bell peppers, deseeded and cut into thin strips
- 3 pounds boneless chicken breast, cut into strips
- Salt and pepper to taste
- 1 can coconut milk
- 1 ½ pounds potatoes, quartered
- 1 tablespoon fish sauce
- 1 tablespoon soy sauce
- 1 tablespoon brown sugar
- Juice from 1 lime, freshly squeezed
- 1 zucchini, sliced

Instructions

1. Press that sauté button on the Instant Pot and heat the oil.
2. Sauté the onion, garlic, and ginger. Stir for a minute until the spices are translucent.

3. Stir in the curry paste, red bell peppers, and chicken.
4. Add in the coconut milk and the rest of the ingredients.
5. Close the lid and press the Poultry button.
6. Cook for 20 minutes.
7. Do natural pressure release.

Nutrition information: Calories per serving: 312; Carbohydrates:19.8 g; Protein:41.2 g; Fat:7.1 g; Sugar: 5.2g; Sodium: 759mg; Fiber: 6.1g

Chicken Moo Goo Gai Pan

Serves: 4
Preparation Time: 5 minutes
Cook Time: 8 minutes

Ingredients

- 1 tablespoon olive oil
- 2 cloves of garlic, minced
- 1-inch fresh ginger, grated
- 1-pound chicken thighs
- ¾ cup chicken stock
- 1 ½ tablespoons soy sauce
- 1 tablespoon dry sherry
- 1 large carrot, sliced thinly
- 1 can button mushrooms
- 1 cup snow peas
- 1 can bamboo shoots
- 1 can water chestnuts

Instructions

1. Press the sauté button on the Instant Pot and heat the oil.
2. Stir in the garlic and ginger. Add in the chicken thighs and continue cooking until the chicken is slightly brown.
3. Add the rest of the ingredients and close the lid.
4. Press the Poultry button and adjust the cooking time to 8 minutes.

5. Do natural pressure release.

Nutrition information: Calories per serving: 269; Carbohydrates: 18g; Protein: 27g; Fat: 9g; Sugar: 6g; Sodium: 567mg; Fiber: 3g

Hoisin Peanut Chicken

Serves: 3
Preparation Time: 5 minutes
Cook Time: 10 minutes

Ingredients

- 1 tablespoon cooking oil
- 2 cloves of garlic, chopped
- ½ teaspoon ginger, grated
- 5 boneless chicken thighs
- ½ cup hoisin
- ¾ cup water
- 3 tablespoons peanut butter
- 1 tablespoon vinegar
- 2 tablespoons sesame oil
- ¼ cup peanut, crushed

Instructions

1. Press the sauté button on the Instant Pot and warm the cooking oil.
2. Sauté the garlic for a z until fragrant. Add the ginger and chicken.
3. Continue stirring until the chicken has browned a little bit.
4. Add the hoisin sauce, water, peanut butter, and vinegar.
5. Close the lid and press the poultry button.
6. Adjust the cooking time to 10 minutes.

7. Do natural pressure release.
8. Once opened, stir in the sesame oil and peanut.

Nutrition information: Calories per serving: 435; Carbohydrates: 5.3g; Protein: 67.7g; Fat: 25.2g; Sugar: 3.2g; Sodium: 743mg; Fiber:0.7 g

Instant Pot Garlic Chicken

Serves: 8

Preparation Time: 10 minutes

Cook Time: 10 minutes

Ingredients

- 8 chicken thighs
- Salt and pepper to taste
- 1 tablespoon olive oil
- 40 cloves of garlic, peeled
- ½ cup chicken stock
- ½ cup white wine
- 1 tablespoon thyme leaves

Instructions

1. Season the chicken thighs with salt and pepper to taste.
2. Press the sauté button and heat the oil.
3. Sauté the chicken thighs and garlic until slightly browned.
4. Pour in the rest of the ingredients.
5. Close the lid and press the Poultry button.
6. Adjust the cooking time to 10 minutes.
7. Do natural pressure release.

Nutrition information: Calories per serving: 473; Carbohydrates:6.74 g; Protein: 33.42g; Fat: 34.02g; Sugar:2.4 g; Sodium: 729mg; Fiber: 1.2g

Salted Instant Pot Baked Chicken

Serves: 5
Preparation Time: 5 minutes
Cook Time: 25 minutes

Ingredients

- 8 chicken legs
- 2 teaspoon ginger powder
- 1 14 teaspoon salt
- ¼ teaspoon five spice powder

Instructions

1. Place all ingredients in the Instant Pot.
2. Close the lid and press the Poultry button.
3. Adjust the cooking time to 25 minutes.

Nutrition information: Calories per serving: 510; Carbohydrates: 0.24 g; Protein: 81.23 g; Fat: 17.27g; Sugar: 0.1 g; Sodium: 532mg; Fiber: 0g

Jamaican Jerk Chicken

Serves: 6
Preparation Time: 2 hours
Cook Time: 25 minutes

Ingredients

- ½ cup organic ketchup
- ¼ cup dark brown sugar
- ¼ cup red wine vinegar
- 3 tablespoon soy sauce
- 2 tablespoon Jamaican jerk seasoning
- 1 teaspoon salt
- 6 chicken drumsticks

Instructions

1. In a mixing bowl, combine the ingredients and allow to marinate for at least 2 hours in the fridge.
2. Pour the marinated chicken in the Instant Pot.
3. Close the lid and press the Poultry button.
4. Cook for 25 minutes.
5. Do quick pressure release.

Nutrition information: Calories per serving: 209; Carbohydrates: 9g; Protein: 11g; Fat: 3g; Sugar: 5g; Sodium: 1139 mg; Fiber: 3g

Pressure Cooker Polynesian Chicken

Serves: 8
Preparation Time: 5 minutes
Cook Time: 15 minutes

Ingredients

- 6 chicken breasts, skin and bone removed
- Juice from 3 oranges, freshly squeezed
- 2 tablespoon lemon juice
- 1 teaspoon soy sauce
- 1 peach, sliced
- 1 cup pineapple chunks

Instructions

1. Place all ingredients in the Instant Pot.
2. Close the lid and press the Poultry button.
3. Adjust the cooking time to 15 minutes.
4. Do natural pressure release.

Nutrition information: Calories per serving: 403; Carbohydrates:7.23 g; Protein:45.5 g; Fat: 20.3g; Sugar: 2.3g; Sodium: 458mg; Fiber: 12g

Tandoori Chicken

Serves: 6
Preparation Time: 5 minutes
Cook Time: 35 minutes

Ingredients

- 1 tablespoon coconut oil
- 3 cloves of garlic, minced
- ½ onion minced
- 3 large chicken breasts
- ½ cup water
- 1 can coconut milk
- 2 teaspoons smoked paprika
- 1 teaspoon turmeric
- 1 ½ teaspoon ground cumin
- 1 ½ teaspoon black pepper
- 1 teaspoon cayenne pepper
- Salt to taste

Instructions

1. Press the sauté button and heat the oil.
2. Sauté the garlic and onion until fragrant and translucent.
3. Add in the chicken breasts and sear all sides until slightly browned.
4. Pour in the rest of the ingredients.
5. Close the lid and press the Poultry button.
6. Cook for 35 minutes

Nutrition information: Calories per serving: 260; Carbohydrates: 9.7 g; Protein: 9.09g; Fat: 22.38g; Sugar: 3.1g; Sodium: 683mg; Fiber: 2.8g

Chinese Orange Chicken

Serves: 6
Preparation Time: 5 minutes
Cook Time: 25 minutes

Ingredients

- 4 boneless chicken breasts
- 1/3 cup water
- ¼ cup soy sauce
- 2 tablespoon brown sugar
- 1 tablespoon red wine vinegar
- ½ teaspoon chili powder
- 1 teaspoon salt
- 1 teaspoon pepper
- ½ cup orange marmalade
- 4 tablespoons water

Instructions

1. Place all ingredients in the Instant Pot.
2. Close the lid and press the Poultry button.
3. Adjust the cooking time for 25 minutes.

Nutrition information: Calories per serving: 326; Carbohydrates: 23.5 g; Protein: 41.82 g; Fat: 6.7g; Sugar: 15.2g; Sodium: 691mg; Fiber: 4.3g

Chapter 5: Vegetarian-Approved Whole Food Instant Pot Recipes

Instant Pot Mashed Potatoes

Serves: 8
Preparation Time: 10 minutes
Cook Time: 25 minutes

Ingredients

- 3 pounds potatoes, peeled and halved
- 1 ½ cups vegetable stock
- ¾ teaspoon salt
- Fresh ground black pepper
- 3 tablespoons olive oil
- ¾ cup heavy cream
- A sprig of rosemary, minced

Instructions

1. Place the potatoes and chicken stock in the Instant Pot.
2. Close the lid and press the Manual button.
3. Cook for 25 minutes.
4. Do quick pressure release.
5. Transfer the potatoes in a food processor and pulse until smooth. You can also use a potato masher to mash the potatoes.

6. Place in a mixing bowl and add the remaining ingredients.

Nutrition information: Calories per serving: 563; Carbohydrates: 30.57g; Protein:3.82 g; Fat: 49.52g; Sugar:4.2g; Sodium: 126mg; Fiber: 16.3g

Beet, Cabbage and Apple Stew

Serves: 4
Preparation Time: 5 minutes
Cook Time: 20 minutes

Ingredients

- 4 cups vegetable broth
- 1 apple, diced
- ½ head of cabbage, chopped
- 1 small onion, chopped
- 2 beets, chopped
- 2 small carrots, chopped
- 1 tablespoon ginger, grated
- 2 tablespoons parsley
- Salt to taste

Instructions

1. Place everything in the Instant Pot.
2. Close the lid and press the Manual button.
3. Cook for 20 minutes.
4. Allow to release the pressure naturally.

Nutrition information: Calories per serving: 77; Carbohydrates: 18.92g; Protein: 1.64g; Fat: 0.8g; Sugar: 3.5g; Sodium: 64mg; Fiber:12.6 g

Instant Pot Butternut Squash

Serves: 4
Preparation Time: 5 minutes
Cook Time: 3 minutes

Ingredients

- 2 pounds butternut squash, chopped
- ¾ cup of water
- 1 onion, chopped
- 1 tablespoon pumpkin pie spice
- 1 tablespoon dried oregano
- 1 teaspoon garlic powder
- 1 teaspoon chili powder

Instructions

1. Mix all ingredients in the Instant Pot.
2. Close the lid and press the Manual button.
3. Cook for 3 minutes.

Nutrition information: Calories per serving:122; Carbohydrates: 30.95g; Protein: 2.9g; Fat: 0.53g; Sugar: 3.2g; Sodium: 46mg; Fiber: 23.5g

Artichokes with Lemon and Tarragon Sauce

Serves: 4

Preparation Time: 10 minutes

Cook Time: 20 minutes

Ingredients

- 4 artichokes, rinsed and cleaned
- 2 small lemons
- 2 cups vegetable broth
- 1 tablespoon tarragon leaves, chopped
- 1 stalk celery
- ½ cup extra virgin olive oil
- Salt to taste

Instructions

1. Place the artichokes in the Instant Pot.
2. Zest the lemon then set it aside. Stir in the lemon zest into the Instant Pot.
3. Pour in the broth.
4. Close the lid and press the Manual button. Cook for 20 minutes.
5. Meanwhile, chop the lemon fruit and remove the seed. Place in the food processor along with the rest of the ingredients. Pulse until slightly smooth.
6. Serve artichokes with the dipping sauce.

Nutrition information: Calories per serving: 194; Carbohydrates: 20.54g; Protein: 5.6g; Fat: 11.94g; Sugar: 5.2g; Sodium: 137mg; Fiber: 10.8 g

Tomato Basil Soup

Serves: 4
Preparation Time: 5 minutes
Cook Time: 30 minutes

Ingredients

- 2 tablespoons olive oil
- 1 onion, chopped
- 3 pounds ripe tomatoes, quartered
- 2 tablespoons tomato paste
- ½ cup fresh basil leaves
- 4 drops of Tabasco sauce
- 3 cups vegetable stock
- ¼ cup coconut milk
- Salt and pepper to taste

Instructions

1. Press the Sauté button in the Instant Pot.
2. Heat the oil and sauté the olive oil until translucent.
3. Add the tomatoes and tomato paste.
4. Stir in the basil and Tabasco sauce.
5. Pour in the vegetable stock.
6. Close the lid and press the Manual button.
7. Cook for 15 minutes.
8. Do quick pressure release to open the lid.
9. Add the coconut milk and season with salt and pepper.

10. Close the lid and continue cooking for another 15 minutes.

Nutrition information: Calories per serving: 244; Carbohydrates: 30.1g; Protein: 7.41g; Fat: 12.62g; Sugar: 3.2g; Sodium: 133mg; Fiber: 23.6g

Curried Broccoli Cream Soup

Serves: 5
Preparation Time: 5 minutes
Cook Time: 5 minutes

Ingredients

- 2 tablespoons olive oil
- 3 medium leeks, white part only
- 2 medium shallots, chopped
- 1 tablespoon Indian curry powder
- Salt and pepper to taste
- 1 ½ pounds broccoli, chopped into florets
- ¼ cup apple, peeled and diced
- 4 cups vegetable broth
- 1 cup coconut milk

Instructions

1. Press the sauté button on the Instant Pot and warm the oil
2. Sauté the leeks and shallots until translucent. Stir in the curry powder and season with salt and pepper to taste.
3. Stir in the broccoli and apples.
4. Pour in the vegetable broth and coconut milk.
5. Close the lid and press the Manual button.
6. Cook for 5 minutes.

Nutrition information: Calories per serving: 243; Carbohydrates: 19.48g; Protein: 6.69g; Fat: 17.88g; Sugar: 3.6g; Sodium: 275mg; Fiber: 13.2g

Instant Pot Brussels Sprouts

Serves: 5
Preparation Time: 5 minutes
Cook Time: 10 minutes

Ingredients

- 1-pound Brussels sprouts
- ¼ cup pine nuts, toasted
- 1 pomegranate, seeds reserved
- 1 tablespoon olive oil
- Salt and pepper to taste

Instructions

1. Place a steam rack in the Instant Pot. Pour water and set it aside.
2. Place the Brussels sprouts on the steam rack.
3. Close the lid and press the Steam button.
4. Cook for 3 minutes.
5. Once done, do quick pressure release.
6. Place the steamed broccoli in a mixing bowl and stir in pine nuts, pomegranate seeds, and olive oil.
7. Season with salt and pepper to taste.

Nutrition information: Calories per serving: 159; Carbohydrates: 20.4g; Protein: 5.11g; Fat: 8.27g; Sugar: 4.2g; Sodium: 164mg; Fiber: 10.6 g

Instant Pot Braised Kale and Carrots

Serves: 3
Preparation Time: 5 minutes
Cook Time: 5 minutes

Ingredients

- 1 tablespoon olive oil
- 1 medium onion, sliced
- 5 cloves of garlic, peeled and chopped
- 10 ounces of kale, cleaned and chopped
- 3 medium carrots, sliced
- ½ cup vegetable broth
- Salt and pepper to taste
- Aged balsamic vinegar

Instructions

1. Press the sauté button on the Instant Pot.
2. Place the olive oil and sauté the onion and garlic until translucent.
3. Add the rest of the ingredients.
4. Close the lid and press the Manual button.
5. Cook for 3 minutes.
6. Do quick pressure release.

Nutrition information: Calories per serving: 104; Carbohydrates: 12.41g; Protein: 4.72g; Fat: 5.44 g; Sugar: 3.5g; Sodium: 175mg; Fiber: 5.7 g

Moroccan Spiced Potatoes

Serves: 6
Preparation Time: 5 minutes
Cook Time: 15 minutes

Ingredients

- 2 tablespoons coconut oil
- 1-pound yellow potatoes, skin removed
- 1 ½ Moroccan spice mix
- Juice from ½ lemon, freshly squeezed
- 1 cup water

Instructions

1. Press the sauté button in the Instant Pot.
2. Heat the oil and stir in the potatoes. Stir for a minute.
3. Pour the rest of the ingredients.
4. Close the lid and press the Manual button.
5. Cook for 15 minutes.
6. Do natural pressure release.

Nutrition information: Calories per serving: 162; Carbohydrates: 19.18 g; Protein: 1.88g; Fat: 9g; Sugar: 2.7g; Sodium: 341mg; Fiber: 7.1g

Instant Pot Baked Potatoes

Serves: 8
Preparation Time: 5 minutes
Cook Time: 10 minutes

Ingredients

- 2 pounds of potatoes, scrubbed
- Salt and pepper to taste

Instructions

1. Pour a cup of water in the Instant Pot.
2. Place a steam rack.
3. Season the potatoes with salt and pepper.
4. Add any spices that you like.
5. Place the potatoes on the steam rack.
6. Close the lid and press the Steam button.
7. Adjust the cooking time to 10 minutes.

Nutrition information: Calories per serving: 90; Carbohydrates: 20.34g; Protein: 2.4g; Fat: 0.11g; Sugar: 2g; Sodium: 132mg; Fiber: 13.6g

Easy Steamed Butternut Squash

Serves: 4
Preparation Time: 5 minutes
Cook Time: 10 minutes

Ingredients

- 1 large butternut squash, halved and deseeded
- Salt and pepper to taste
- A dash of olive oil

Instructions

1. Pour a cup of water in the Instant Pot.
2. Place a steam rack.
3. Season the squash with salt and pepper.
4. Add a dash of olive oil.
5. Add any spices that you like.
6. Place the potatoes on the steam rack.
7. Close the lid and press the Steam button.
8. Adjust the cooking time to 10 minutes.

Nutrition information: Calories per serving: 47; Carbohydrates: 3.77g; Protein: 1.2g; Fat: 3.4g; Sugar: 0.8g; Sodium: 23mg; Fiber: 0.5g

Instant Pot Seasoned Cauliflower

Serves: 4

Preparation Time: 1 hour

Cook Time: 5 minutes

Ingredients

- 1 medium head of cauliflower, cut into florets
- 2 tablespoons olive oil
- ¼ teaspoon salt
- ½ teaspoon dried parsley
- ¼ teaspoon cumin
- ¼ teaspoon turmeric
- ¼ teaspoon paprika
- Cilantro, for garnish

Instructions

1. In a mixing bowl, combine all ingredients except the cilantro together.
2. Marinate in the fridge for at least an hour.
3. Pour a cup of water in the Instant Pot.
4. Place a steam rack.
5. Place the cauliflower on the steam rack.
6. Close the lid and press the Steam button.
7. Adjust the cooking time to 5 minutes.
8. Do quick pressure release.
9. Garnish with cilantro.

Nutrition information: Calories per serving: 78; Carbohydrates:3.57 g; Protein: 1.34g; Fat: 6.99g; Sugar: 0g; Sodium: 56mg; Fiber: 2.1g

Crispy Potatoes in Instant Pot

Serves: 4
Preparation Time: 5 minutes
Cook Time: 15 minutes

Ingredients

- 1-pound Yukon Gold potatoes, cubed
- 2 tablespoons coconut oil
- Salt and pepper to taste
- ¼ cup Italian parsley, minced
- Juice from ½ lemon, freshly squeezed
- 4 tablespoons water

Instructions

1. Mix all ingredients in a mixing bowl.
2. Place the potatoes in the Instant Pot.
3. Close the lid and press the Manual button.
4. Cook for 15 minutes on low pressure.

Nutrition information: Calories per serving: 153; Carbohydrates: 21.3 g; Protein: 2.6g; Fat: 6.97g; Sugar: 2.4g; Sodium: 231mg; Fiber: 14.7g

Butternut Squash and Apples

Serves: 6
Preparation Time: 5 minutes
Cook Time: 15 minutes

Ingredients

- 1 tablespoon olive oil
- 1 butternut squash, peeled and cut into cubes
- 1 apple, peeled and cubed
- 1 teaspoon ginger powder
- 4 cups vegetable broth
- Olive oil for drizzling

Instructions

1. Press the sauté button on Instant Pot.
2. Heat the olive oil and add the butternut squash. Brown the squash lightly for 5 minutes.
3. Add the apples and the rest of the ingredients except the olive oil.
4. Close the Instant Pot.
5. Press the Manual button and cook for 10 minutes.
6. Do quick pressure release.
7. Drizzle with olive oil before serving.

Nutrition information: Calories per serving: 326; Carbohydrates: 53.9g; Protein: 1.9g; Fat: 13.96g; Sugar: 2.1g; Sodium: 328mg; Fiber: 30.2g

Creamed Fennel and Cauliflower Soup

Serves: 4
Preparation Time: 5 minutes
Cook Time: 15 minutes

Ingredients

- 1 tablespoon coconut oil
- 1 onion, sliced
- 3 cloves of garlic, minced
- 1 large fennel bulbs, cleaned and sliced
- 1-pound cauliflower, sliced into florets
- 1 cup coconut milk
- 3 cups vegetable broth
- Salt and pepper to taste

Instructions

1. Press the sauté button on the Instant Pot.
2. Heat the oil and sauté the onions and garlic until fragrant.
3. Stir in the fennel slices and cauliflower and cook until slightly toasty.
4. Pour in the coconut milk and vegetable broth.
5. Season with salt and pepper to taste.
6. Close the lid and press the Manual button.
7. Cook for 10 minutes.

Nutrition information: Calories per serving: 231; Carbohydrates: 17.5g; Protein: 4.7g; Fat: 18.2g; Sugar: 1.3g; Sodium: 132mg; Fiber: 10.7g

Scrumptious Beefless Stew

Serves: 8

Preparation Time: 5 minutes

Cook Time: 10 minutes

Ingredients

- 1 teaspoon olive oil
- 1 white onion, chopped
- 1 ½ tablespoon chopped garlic
- 3 medium carrots, sliced
- 3 ribs of celery, sliced
- 2 medium mushrooms, cut into pieces
- 5 cups water
- 2 pounds potatoes, peeled and cubed
- 1/3 cup tomato paste
- 1 tablespoon Italian herb seasoning
- 1 tablespoon paprika
- Salt and pepper to taste

Instructions

1. Press the sauté button on the Instant Pot.
2. Heat the olive oil and sauté the onions and garlic until fragrant and translucent.
3. Add the carrots and celery. Cook for a minute more.
4. Stir in the mushroom and the rest of the ingredients.

5. Close the lid and press the Manual button.
6. Cook for 10 minutes.
7. Do natural pressure release.

Nutrition information: Calories per serving: 168; Carbohydrates: 36.9 g; Protein: 6.2g; Fat: 4 g; Sugar: 0.1g; Sodium: 93mg; Fiber: 7.5g

Indian Pickled Potatoes

Serves: 4
Preparation Time: 5 minutes
Cook Time: 10 minutes

Ingredients

- 4 tablespoons oil
- 1 tablespoon cumin seeds
- 1 tablespoon coriander seeds
- 5 cloves
- 1 bay leaf
- ½ teaspoon red chili powder
- ½ teaspoon turmeric powder
- 1 teaspoon dry pomegranate powder
- 2 teaspoon dried fenugreek leaves
- 1 tablespoon mango pickle
- 1-pound potatoes, cubed

Instructions

1. Press the sauté button on the Instant Pot.
2. Heat the oil and sauté the cumin seeds, coriander seeds, cloves, bay leaf, chili powder, turmeric powder, pomegranate powder, and fenugreek leaves until fragrant.
3. Add the mango pickles and the potatoes.
4. Adjust the amount of liquid by adding 4 tablespoons of water.

5. Close the Instant Pot and press the Manual button.
6. Cook on low pressure for 10 minutes.

Nutrition information: Calories per serving: 288; Carbohydrates: 37g; Protein: 4.4g; Fat: 15.3g; Sugar: 4.2g; Sodium:274 mg; Fiber: 20.7g

Vegan Posole

Serves: 8
Preparation Time: 5 minutes
Cook Time: 40 minutes

Ingredients

- 1 tablespoon oil
- 1 onion, sliced
- 8 garlic cloves, minced
- 2 cans of green jackfruit
- ¼ cup red chili, pureed
- 2 cans organic hominy
- 6 cups vegetable broth

Instructions

1. Set the Instant Pot to sauté.
2. Heat the oil and sauté the onion and garlic.
3. Add the jackfruit and pureed chili. Continue stirring for a few minutes.
4. Add the hominy and vegetable broth.
5. Close the lid and press the Manual button.
6. Adjust the cooking time to 40 minutes.
7. Do quick pressure release.

Nutrition information: Calories per serving: 99; Carbohydrates: 19.1g; Protein: 1.6g; Fat: 2.4g; Sugar: 2.4g; Sodium: 381mg; Fiber: 13.9g

Instant Pot Refried Beans

Serves: 6
Preparation Time: 10 minutes
Cook Time: 40 minutes

Ingredients

- 2 pounds dried pinto beans, sorted
- 3 tablespoons coconut oil
- 1 ½ cups chopped onions
- 5 cloves of garlic, minced
- 2 teaspoon dried oregano
- 1 ½ teaspoon ground cumin
- 1 jalapeno, seeded and chopped
- 4 cups vegetable broth
- 4 cups water
- Salt and pepper to taste

Instructions

1. In a bowl, soak the pinto beans in water. Set aside.
2. Press the sauté button on the Instant Pot and heat the oil.
3. Sauté the onions and garlic until they are fragrant and translucent.
4. Stir in the oregano, cumin, and jalapeno.
5. Pour in the vegetable broth and water.
6. Add in the beans. Season with salt and pepper to taste.
7. Close the lid and press the Manual button.

8. Adjust the cooking time to 40 minutes.

Nutrition information: Calories per serving: 612; Carbohydrates: 100.2g; Protein: 33.76g; Fat: 8.85g; Sugar: 2.8g; Sodium: 312mg; Fiber: 80.3g

Lentil Bolognese

Serves: 6
Preparation Time: 5 minutes
Cook Time: 30 minutes

Ingredients

- 2 tablespoons olive oil
- 1 onion, chopped
- 7 cloves of garlic, minced
- 1 rib celery, chopped
- 3 large carrots, chopped
- ½ cup of tomato sauce
- ¼ cup tomato paste
- 2 cups Italian tomatoes
- 2 tablespoon dried sweet basil
- 1 teaspoon dried oregano
- 2 cups red lentils
- 2 cups water
- Salt and pepper to taste

Instructions

1. Press the sauté button and heat the oil.
2. Sauté the onion and garlic until fragrant and translucent.
3. Add the celery and carrots. Cook for another minute.
4. Stir in the rest of the ingredients.
5. Close the lid and press the Manual button.

6. Cook for 30 minutes or until the lentils are soft.
7. Do natural pressure release.

Nutrition information: Calories per serving: 340; Carbohydrates: 55.75g; Protein: 17.73g; Fat: 6.25g; Sugar: 4.7g; Sodium: 654mg; Fiber: 37.9g

60597762R10082

Made in the USA
Middletown, DE
02 January 2018